LIMITLESS

TRAINING JOURNAL

This book belongs to:

TABLE OF CONTENTS

INTRODUCTION

What is CrossFit?

CrossFit is a strength and conditioning program that is broad, general and scalable for all ages and athletic abilities. CrossFit workouts are comprised of constantly varied functional movements (like running, jumping, pushing, pulling, squatting, lifting, climbing...) performed at high intensity.

What is Fitness?

CrossFit uses three standards to define fitness.

1. **10 General Physical Skills** – An individual's fitness level is defined by their competence in each skill.
   - **Cardiovascular endurance** – The ability of the body to gather, process, and deliver oxygen.
   - **Stamina** – The ability of the body to process, deliver, store and utilize energy.
   - **Strength** – The ability of a muscular unit, or combination of muscular units, to apply force.
   - **Flexibility** – The ability to maximize the range of motion of a given joint.
   - **Power** – The ability of a muscular unit, or combination of units, to apply maximum force in minimum time.
   - **Speed** – The ability to minimize the time cycle of a repeated movement.
   - **Coordination** – The ability to combine several distinct movement patterns into a singular distinct movement.
   - **Agility** – The ability to minimize transition time from one distinct movement pattern to another.
   - **Balance** – The ability to control the placement of the body's center of gravity in relation to its support base.

- **Accuracy** – The ability to control movement in a given direction or at a given intensity.

2. **Hopper Method** - An individual's capacity to perform well at any given task regardless of the weight, repetitions, sequence or environmental conditions.

3. **Energy Pathways** – There are three metabolic pathways that provide energy to the human body. An individual's fitness level is defined by their competency in all three pathways.

   - Phosphagen – Activity lasting less than 10 seconds.
   - Glycolytic – Activity lasting up to several minutes.
   - Oxidative – Low powered activity lasting in excess of several minutes.

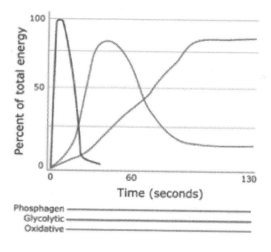

Content based on CrossFit Journal October 2002. For more information visit www.CrossFit.com

PHYSICAL ASSESSMENT

	Day 1	Day 30	Day 60	Day 90	Goal
Actual Date:					
Body Weight:					
Body Fat%:					
Measurements					
Neck					
Shoulders					
Chest					
Bicep – R					
Bicep – L					
Waist					
Hips					
Mid-Thigh – R					
Mid-Thigh – L					
Calf – R					
Calf – L					

Benchmarks

Fran				
Helen				
Diane				

Max Lifts

Snatch				
C&J				
Front Squat				
Back Squat				
Deadlift				
Weighted Pullup				
Push Press				

Bodyweight

Muscle Ups				
Pullups				
Ring Dips				
HSPU				

Conditioning

400M Run				
Mile Run				
5K Run				
2000M Row				

HOW TO USE THIS BOOK

Enter personal records (PR) in the Personal Best section. This is an easy way to track your strength gains.

Enter your workout details in the "Workout of the Day" section *immediately* after each training session. If you wait, you will forget.

After each WOD enter your M = Mood, F = Fatigue, and S = Soreness on a scale of 1-10 with 10 being bad and 1 being ideal. This will help prevent you from overtraining.

Be sure to enter Girl named bench marks in their proper areas to track your metabolic improvements.

Start out by filling in the information and then show your tracking log to your coach for guidance on how to improve when you're ready.

This book is best used with our, *CFL Nutrition Guide for CrossFit Athletes*, available on Amazon.com

1. General warm-up - 5 minutes (i.e. Row 500M, Run 400M or Jump Rope for 5 minutes.)
2. Mobility work – 10 minutes (i.e. Foam roller, lacrosse ball, or band stretches.)
3. Movement specific warm-up – 5 minutes (Light weight reps of the exercises you will be performing.)
4. WOD
5. Range of motion stretching - 10 minutes (Increase your range of motion after your workout while your muscles are warm and pliable.)

Date:	M/F/S:

Date:	M/F/S:

Date:	M/F/S:
Date:	M/F/S:

Date:	M/F/S:

Date:	M/F/S:

| Date: | M/F/S: |
| | |

| Date: | M/F/S: |
| | |

| Date: | M/F/S: |
| | |

| Date: | M/F/S: |
| | |

Date: M/F/S:

Date: M/F/S:

Date: M/F/S:

Date: M/F/S:

Date: M/F/S:

Date: M/F/S:

Date:	M/F/S:

Date:	M/F/S:

Date:	M/F/S:

Date:	M/F/S:

Date: | M/F/S:

Date: | M/F/S:

Date: M/F/S:

Date: M/F/S:

Date:	M/F/S:

Date:	M/F/S:

Date: M/F/S:

Date: M/F/S:

Date: M/F/S:

Date: M/F/S:

Date:	M/F/S:
Date:	M/F/S:

Date:	M/F/S:

Date:	M/F/S:

Date:	M/F/S:
Date:	M/F/S:

27

Date:	M/F/S:

Date:	M/F/S:

Date:	M/F/S:

Date:	M/F/S:

Date:	M/F/S:

Date:	M/F/S:

Date:	M/F/S:

Date:	M/F/S:

Date: M/F/S:

Date: M/F/S:

Date:	M/F/S:

Date:	M/F/S:

Date: M/F/S:

Date: M/F/S:

Date:	M/F/S:

Date:	M/F/S:

Date:	M/F/S:

Date:	M/F/S:

Date:	M/F/S:
Date:	M/F/S:

Date:	M/F/S:

Date:	M/F/S:

Date:	M/F/S:

Date:	M/F/S:

Date:	M/F/S:

Date:	M/F/S:

Date:	M/F/S:

Date:	M/F/S:

Date:	M/F/S:

Date:	M/F/S:

Date:	M/F/S:

Date:	M/F/S:

Date: M/F/S:

Date: M/F/S:

Date:	M/F/S:
Date:	M/F/S:

Date:	M/F/S:

Date:	M/F/S:

Date:	M/F/S:

Date:	M/F/S:

Date:	M/F/S:

Date:	M/F/S:

Date:	M/F/S:

Date:	M/F/S:

Date: M/F/S:

Date: M/F/S:

Date: M/F/S:

Date: M/F/S:

Date: M/F/S:

Date: M/F/S:

Date:	M/F/S:

Date:	M/F/S:

Date:	M/F/S:

Date:	M/F/S:

Date: M/F/S:

Date: M/F/S:

Date:	M/F/S:

Date:	M/F/S:

Date:	M/F/S:

Date:	M/F/S:

Date:	M/F/S:

Date:	M/F/S:

Date:	M/F/S:
Date:	M/F/S:

Date:	M/F/S:

Date:	M/F/S:

Date:	M/F/S:

Date:	M/F/S:

Date:	M/F/S:

Date:	M/F/S:

Date:	M/F/S:

Date:	M/F/S:

Date:	M/F/S:

Date:	M/F/S:

Date:	M/F/S:

Date:	M/F/S:

Date: M/F/S:

Date: M/F/S:

Date:	M/F/S:

Date:	M/F/S:

Date:	M/F/S:

Date:	M/F/S:

Date: | M/F/S:

Date: | M/F/S:

Date: M/F/S:

Date: M/F/S:

Date: M/F/S:

Date: M/F/S:

Date: | M/F/S:

Date: | M/F/S:

Date: M/F/S:

Date: M/F/S:

Date:	M/F/S:

Date:	M/F/S:

Date: | M/F/S:

Date: | M/F/S:

Date: M/F/S:

Date: M/F/S:

76

Date:	M/F/S:

Date:	M/F/S:

Date: M/F/S:

Date: M/F/S:

Date:

M/F/S:

Date:

M/F/S:

Date:	M/F/S:

Date:	M/F/S:

Date:	M/F/S:
Date:	M/F/S:

Date:	M/F/S:

Date:	M/F/S:

Date:	M/F/S:

Date:	M/F/S:

Date:	M/F/S:

Date:	M/F/S:

Date:	M/F/S:

Date:	M/F/S:

Date: | M/F/S:

Date: | M/F/S:

Date:	M/F/S:

Date:	M/F/S:

Date:	M/F/S:
Date:	M/F/S:

Date:	M/F/S:

Date:	M/F/S:

Date:	M/F/S:

Date:	M/F/S:

Date:	M/F/S:

Date:	M/F/S:

Date:	M/F/S:

Date:	M/F/S:

Date:	M/F/S:

Date:	M/F/S:

Date:	M/F/S:

Date:	M/F/S:

Date:	M/F/S:

Date:	M/F/S:

Date: M/F/S:

Date: M/F/S:

96

Date:	M/F/S:

Date:	M/F/S:

Date: M/F/S:

Date: M/F/S:

98

Date:	M/F/S:

Date:	M/F/S:

Date:	M/F/S:

Date:	M/F/S:

Date:	M/F/S:

Date:	M/F/S:

Date:	M/F/S:

Date:	M/F/S:

Date:	M/F/S:

Date:	M/F/S:

Date: M/F/S:

Date: M/F/S:

Date:	M/F/S:

Date:	M/F/S:

Date:	M/F/S:

Date:	M/F/S:

Date: M/F/S:

Date: M/F/S:

Date: M/F/S:

Date: M/F/S:

Date: M/F/S:

Date: M/F/S:

Date:	M/F/S:

Date:	M/F/S:

Date:

M/F/S:

Date:

M/F/S:

Date: M/F/S:

Date: M/F/S:

Date:	M/F/S:

Date:	M/F/S:

Date: M/F/S:

Date: M/F/S:

Date:	M/F/S:

Date:	M/F/S:

Date:	M/F/S:

Date:	M/F/S:

Date: | M/F/S:

Date: | M/F/S:

Date:	M/F/S:

Date:	M/F/S:

Date:	M/F/S:

Date:	M/F/S:

Date:	M/F/S:

Date:	M/F/S:

Date:	M/F/S:

Date:	M/F/S:

Date:	M/F/S:

Date:	M/F/S:

Date: M/F/S:

Date: M/F/S:

Date: M/F/S:

Date: M/F/S:

Date: M/F/S:

Date: M/F/S:

125

Date: M/F/S:

Date: M/F/S:

Date:	M/F/S:

Date:	M/F/S:

Date:	M/F/S:

Date:	M/F/S:

Date:	M/F/S:

Date:	M/F/S:

Date: M/F/S:

Date: M/F/S:

Date:	M/F/S:

Date:	M/F/S:

Date: | M/F/S:

Date: | M/F/S:

Date:	M/F/S:

Date:	M/F/S:

Date: M/F/S:

Date: M/F/S:

Date:	M/F/S:

Date:	M/F/S:

Date:	M/F/S:

Date:	M/F/S:

Date:	M/F/S:

Date:	M/F/S:

Date: M/F/S:

Date: M/F/S:

138

Date: M/F/S:

Date: M/F/S:

Date: M/F/S:

Date: M/F/S:

140

Date:	M/F/S:

Date:	M/F/S:

Date: | M/F/S:

Date: | M/F/S:

Date: M/F/S:

Date: M/F/S:

Date:	M/F/S:

Date:	M/F/S:

| Date: | M/F/S: |
| | |

| Date: | M/F/S: |
| | |

Date: M/F/S:

Date: M/F/S:

Date: M/F/S:

Date: M/F/S:

Date:	M/F/S:

Date:	M/F/S:

Date:	M/F/S:

Date:	M/F/S:

Date: M/F/S:

Date: M/F/S:

150

Date: M/F/S:

Date: M/F/S:

151

Date:	M/F/S:

Date:	M/F/S:

Date: | M/F/S:

Date: | M/F/S:

Date:	M/F/S:

Date:	M/F/S:

Date: | M/F/S:

Date: | M/F/S:

Date:

M/F/S:

Date:

M/F/S:

Date: M/F/S:

Date: M/F/S:

Date: M/F/S:

Date: M/F/S:

158

Date:	M/F/S:

Date:	M/F/S:

Date: M/F/S:

Date: M/F/S:

160

Date: M/F/S:

Date: M/F/S:

Date: M/F/S:

Date: M/F/S:

Date: M/F/S:

Date: M/F/S:

Date: M/F/S:

Date: M/F/S:

Date: M/F/S:

Date: M/F/S:

Date: M/F/S:

Date: M/F/S:

Date: | M/F/S:

Date: | M/F/S:

Date:

M/F/S:

Date:

M/F/S:

Date: M/F/S:

Date: M/F/S:

Date: | M/F/S:

Date: | M/F/S:

Date:	M/F/S:

Date:	M/F/S:

PERSONAL BESTS

Back Squat

Date	Weight	Notes

Front Squat

Date	Weight	Notes

Overhead Squat

Date	Weight	Notes

Shoulder Press

Date	Weight	Notes

Push Press

Date	Weight	Notes

Push Jerk

Date	Weight	Notes

Deadlift

Date	Weight	Notes

Clean

Date	Weight	Notes

Clean & Jerk

Date	Weight	Notes

Snatch

Date	Weight	Notes

Bench Press

Date	Weight	Notes

Thruster

Date	Weight	Notes

Pull-Ups (Reps)

Date	Reps	Notes

Weighted Pull-Ups

Date	Weight	Notes

Weighted Dips

Date	Weight	Notes

5K Run

Date	Time	Notes

10K run

Date	Weight	Notes

2K Row

Date	Weight	Notes

Date	Time/Weight/Reps	Notes

Date	Time/Weight/Reps	Notes

Date	Time/Weight/Reps	Notes

Date	Time/Weight/Reps	Notes

Date	Time/Weight/Reps	Notes

Date	Time/Weight/Reps	Notes

Date	Time/Weight/Reps	Notes

Date	Time/Weight/Reps	Notes

Date	Time/Weight/Reps	Notes

GIRL BENCHMARK WODS

Angie	Date	Time	Notes
For Time: 100 Pull-Ups 100 Push-Ups 100 Sit-Ups 100 Squats			

Annie	Date	Time	Notes
50-40-30-20-10 rep rounds for time: Double-Unders Sit-Ups			

Barbara	Date	Time	Notes
5 rounds with 3 minutes rest: 20 pull-ups 30 pushups 40 sit-ups 50 squats			

Chelsea	Date	Time	Notes
Each minute on the minute for 30 minutes: 5 pull-ups 10 pushups 15 squats			

Cindy	Date	Score	Notes
Total rounds in 20 minutes: 5 pull-ups 10 pushups 15 squats			

Diane	Date	Time	Notes
For time: 21-15-9 Deadlift 225 lbs. Handstand pushups			

Elizabeth	Date	Time	Notes
For time: 21-15-9 Clean 135 lbs. Ring dips			

Eva	Date	Time	Notes
5 rounds for time: Run 800 meters 2 pood KB swing, 30 reps 30 pull-ups			

Fran	Date	Time	Notes
For time: 21-15-9 Thruster 95 lbs. Pull-ups			

GI Jane	Date	Time	Notes
100 Reps for time: Burpee-Pull-ups			

Grace	Date	Time	Notes
30 reps for time: Clean and jerk 135 lbs.			

Gwen	Date	Load	Notes
15-12-9 Clean and Jerk Touch and go at floor. No re-grip, no dumping. Rest as needed. Report load.			

Helen	Date	Time	Notes
3 rounds for time: 400 meter run 1.5 kb swing (21 reps) 12 pull-ups			

Isabell	Date	Time	Notes
30 reps for time: Snatch 135 lbs.			

Jackie	Date	Time	Notes
For time: 1000 meter row Thruster 45 lbs. (50 reps) Pull-ups (30 reps)			

Karen	Date	Time	Notes

For time:
150 wall ball shots

Kelly	Date	Time	Notes

5 rounds for time:
Run 400 meters
30 box jump, 24 inch box
30 Wall ball shots, 20 pound ball

Linda	Date	Time	Notes

10-9-8-7-6-5-4-3-2-1 for time:
Clean 3/4 bodyweight
Bench bodyweight
Deadlift 1.5 bodyweight

Lynne	Date	Reps	Notes
5 rounds for max reps: Bench bodyweight Pull-ups			

Mary	Date	Rounds	Notes
AMRAP in 20 minutes: 5 handstand push-ups 10 pistols 15 pull-ups			

Nancy	Date	Time	Notes
5 rounds for time: 400 meter run Overhead squat 95 lbs. (15 reps)			

Nicole	Date	Total Pull-ups	Notes
AMRAP, 20 mins: *Note amount of pull-ups completed* Run 400 meters Max rep Pull-ups			

"Don't wish it were easier. Wish you were better."

~ Jim Rohn

JT	Date	Time	Notes
21-15-9 reps, for time: Handstand push-ups Ring dips Push-ups			

Michael	Date	Time	Notes
3 rounds for time: Run 800 meters 50 Back Extensions 50 Sit-ups			

Murph	Date	Time	Notes
For time. Partition the pull-ups, push-ups, and squats as needed: 1 mile Run 100 Pull-ups 200 Push-ups 300 Squats 1 mile Run			

Daniel	Date	Time	Notes

For time:
50 Pull-ups
400 meter run
95 pound Thruster, 21 reps
800 meter run
95 pound Thruster, 21 reps
400 meter run
50 Pull-ups

Josh	Date	Time	Notes

For time:
95 pound Overhead squat,
21 reps
42 Pull-ups
95 pound Overhead squat,
15 reps
30 Pull-ups
95 pound Overhead squat,
9 reps
18 Pull-ups

Badger	Date	Time	Notes

3 rounds for time:
95 pound Squat clean, 30 reps
30 Pull-ups
Run 800 meters

Nate	Date	Time	Notes
20 Min AMRAP: 2 Muscle-ups 4 Handstand Push-ups 8 2-Pood Kettlebell swings			

Randy	Date	Time	Notes
For time: 75# power snatch, 75 reps			

Tommy V	Date	Time	Notes
For time:			
115 pound Thruster, 21 reps			
15 ft Rope Climb, 12 ascents			
115 pound Thruster, 15 reps			
15 ft Rope Climb, 9 ascents			
115 pound Thruster, 9 reps			
15 ft Rope Climb, 6 ascents			

BASIC STRENGTH STANDARDS

Press-AdultMen

Body Weight	Un-trained	Novice	Intermediate	Advanced	Elite
114	53	72	90	107	129
123	57	78	98	116	141
132	61	84	105	125	151
148	69	94	119	140	169
165	75	102	129	153	186
181	81	110	138	164	218
198	85	116	146	173	234
220	89	122	155	183	255
242	93	127	159	189	264
275	96	131	164	194	272
319	98	133	167	199	278
320+	100	136	171	203	284

Press-AdultWomen

Body Weight	Un-trained	Novice	Intermediate	Advanced	Elite
97	31	42	50	66	85
105	33	46	53	71	91
114	36	49	58	76	97
123	38	52	61	81	104
132	40	55	65	85	110
148	44	60	72	94	121
165	48	65	77	102	134
181	51	70	83	110	140
198	55	75	83	117	151
199+	58	79	93	123	159

Bench Press -Adult Men

Body Weight	Un-trained	Novice	Intermediate	Advanced	Elite
114	84	107	130	179	222
123	91	116	142	194	242
132	98	125	153	208	260
148	109	140	172	234	291
165	119	152	187	255	319
181	128	164	201	275	343
198	135	173	213	289	362
220	142	183	225	306	381
242	149	190	232	316	395
275	153	196	239	325	407
319	156	199	244	333	416
320+	159	204	248	340	425

Bench Press - Adult Women

Body Weight	Un-trained	Novice	Intermediate	Advanced	Elite
97	49	63	73	94	116
105	53	68	79	102	124
114	57	73	85	109	133
123	60	77	90	116	142
132	64	82	95	122	150
148	70	90	105	135	165
165	76	97	113	146	183
181	81	104	122	158	192
198	88	112	130	167	205
199+	92	118	137	177	217

Power Clean - Adult Men

Body Weight	Un-trained	Novice	Intermediate	Advanced	Elite
114	56	103	125	173	207
123	60	112	137	186	224
132	65	121	148	200	239
148	73	135	166	225	266
165	79	147	180	246	288
181	85	158	194	264	310
198	90	167	205	279	327
220	95	176	217	294	345
242	99	183	224	305	357
275	102	188	230	313	367
319	104	192	235	320	376
320+	106	196	239	327	384

Power Clean - Adult Women

Body Weight	Un-trained	Novice	Intermediate	Advanced	Elite
97	33	61	70	93	117
105	35	66	76	101	125
114	38	70	82	108	135
123	40	74	87	115	143
132	43	79	92	121	152
148	47	87	101	133	167
165	50	93	109	144	184
181	54	100	118	155	193
198	58	108	125	165	207
199+	61	114	132	174	218

Squat - Adult Men

Body Weight	Un-trained	Novice	Intermediate	Advanced	Elite
114	78	144	174	240	320
123	84	155	190	259	346
132	91	168	205	278	369
148	101	188	230	313	410
165	110	204	250	342	445
181	119	220	269	367	479
198	125	232	285	387	504
220	132	244	301	409	532
242	137	255	311	423	551
275	141	261	319	435	567
319	144	267	326	445	580

Squat -Adult Women

Body Weight	Un-trained	Novice	Intermediate	Advanced	Elite
97	46	84	98	129	163
105	49	91	106	140	174
114	53	98	114	150	187
123	56	103	121	160	199
132	59	110	127	168	211
148	65	121	141	185	232
165	70	130	151	200	256
181	75	139	164	215	268
198	81	150	174	229	288
199+	85	158	184	242	303

Deadlift -Adult Men

Body Weight	Un-trained	Novice	Intermediate	Advanced	Elite
114	97	179	204	299	387
123	105	194	222	320	414
132	113	209	239	342	438
148	126	234	269	380	482
165	137	254	293	411	518
181	148	274	315	438	548
198	156	289	333	457	567
220	164	305	351	479	586
242	172	318	363	490	596
275	176	326	373	499	602
319	180	333	381	506	608
320+	183	340	388	512	617

Deadlift -Adult Women

Body Weight	Un-trained	Novice	Intermediate	Advanced	Elite
97	57	105	122	175	232
105	61	114	132	189	242
114	66	122	142	200	253
123	70	129	151	211	263
132	74	137	159	220	273
148	81	151	176	241	295
165	88	162	189	258	319
181	94	174	204	273	329
198	101	187	217	284	349
199+	107	197	229	297	364

CROSSFIT ACRONYMS AND ABBREVIATIONS

- **#:** Pounds
- **1RM, 2RM, etc:** Refers to 1 rep max attempt, 3 rep max, etc.
- **AMRAP:** As Many Reps (sometimes Rounds)as Possible
- **BB:** Barbell
- **BP:** Bench press
- **BS:** Back squat (assume low bar back squat unless stated otherwise)
- **BW:** Body weight
- **CFT:** CrossFit Total - consisting of max squat, press, and deadlift.
- **CFWU:** CrossFit Warm-up
- **CLN:** Clean
- **C&J:** Clean and jerk
- **C2:** Concept II rowing machine
- **DB:** Dumbbell
- **DL:** Deadlift
- **FS:** Front squat
- **GHR(D):** Glute ham raise (developer). Posterior chain exercise, like a back extension. Also, the device that allows for the proper performance of a GHR.
- **GHR(D) Sit-up:** Sit-up done on the GHR(D) bench.
- **GPP:** General physical preparedness, aka "fitness."
- **H2H:** Hand to hand; refers to Jeff Martone's kettlebell "juggling" techniques (or to combat).
- **HBBS:** High bar back squat. Bar is placed on traps.
- **HSPU:** Hand stand push up. Kick up into a handstand (use wall for balance, if needed) bend arms until nose touches floor and push back up.
- **HSQ:** Hang squat (clean or snatch). Start with bar "at the hang," about knee height. Initiate pull. As the bar rises drop into a full squat and catch the bar in the racked position. From there, rise to a standing position
- **KB:** Kettlebell
- **KBS:** Kettlebell swings
- **K2E:** Knees to elbows. Similar to T2Bs described below.
- **ME:** Max effort.
- **MetCon:** Metabolic Conditioning workout
- **MP:** Military press

- **MU**: Muscle ups. Hanging from rings you do a combination pull-up and dip so you end in an upright support.
- **OHS**: Overhead squat. Full-depth squat performed while arms are locked out in a wide grip press position above (and usually behind) the head.
- **PC**: Power clean
- **Pd**: Pood, weight measure for kettlebells. 1 Pood ~ 35lbs.
- **PR**: Personal record
- **PP**: Push press
- **PSN**: Power snatch
- **PU**: Pull-ups, possibly push-ups, depending on the context
- **Rep**: Repetition. One performance of an exercise.
- **Rx'd; as Rx'd**: As prescribed; as written. WOD done without any adjustments.
- **RM**: Repetition maximum. Your 1RM is your max lift for one rep. Your 10 RM is the most you can lift 10 times.
- **SDHP**: Sumo deadlift high pull (see exercise section)
- **Set**: A number of repetitions. e.g., 3 sets of 10 reps, often seen as 3x10, means do 10 reps, rest, repeat, rest, repeat.
- **SPP**: Specific physical preparedness, aka skill training.
- **SN**: Snatch
- **SQ**: Squat
- **Subbed**: Substituted. The **CORRECT** use of "subbed," as in "substituted," is, "I subbed an exercise I can do for one I can't," For example, if you can't do HSPU, you subbed regular pushups.
- **TGU**: Turkish get-up
- **T2B**: Toes to bar. Hang from bar. Bending only at waist raise your toes to touch the bar, slowly lower them and repeat.
- **UB**: Unbroken (complete set without breaks)
- **WOD**: Workout of the day

> *What lies behind us and what lies before us are tiny matters compared to what lies within us. ~ Ralph Waldo Emerson*

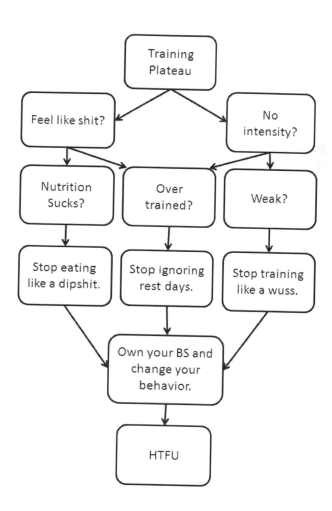

MAX PERCENTAGES

Max Load	55%	60%	65%	70%	75%	80%	85%	90%	95%
75	41	45	49	53	56	60	64	68	71
80	44	48	52	56	60	64	68	72	76
85	47	51	55	60	64	68	72	77	81
90	50	54	59	63	68	72	77	81	86
95	52	57	62	67	71	76	81	86	90
100	55	60	65	70	75	80	85	90	95
105	58	63	68	74	79	84	89	95	100
110	61	66	72	77	83	88	94	99	105
115	63	69	75	81	86	92	98	104	109
120	66	72	78	84	90	96	102	108	114
125	69	75	81	88	94	100	106	113	119
130	72	78	85	91	98	104	111	117	124
135	74	81	88	95	101	108	115	122	128
140	77	84	91	98	105	112	119	126	133
145	80	87	94	102	109	116	123	131	138
150	83	90	98	105	113	120	128	135	143
155	85	93	101	109	116	124	132	140	147
160	88	96	104	112	120	128	136	144	152
165	91	99	107	116	124	132	140	149	157
170	94	102	111	119	128	136	145	153	162
175	96	105	114	123	131	140	149	158	166
180	99	108	117	126	135	144	153	162	171
185	102	111	120	130	139	148	157	167	176
190	105	114	124	133	143	152	162	171	181
195	107	117	127	137	146	156	166	176	185
200	110	120	130	140	150	160	170	180	190
205	113	123	133	144	154	164	174	185	195
210	116	126	137	147	158	168	179	189	200
215	118	129	140	151	161	172	183	194	204

Max Load	55%	60%	65%	70%	75%	80%	85%	90%	95%
220	121	132	143	154	165	176	187	198	209
225	124	135	146	158	169	180	191	203	214
230	127	138	150	161	173	184	196	207	219
235	129	141	153	165	176	188	200	212	223
240	132	144	156	168	180	192	204	216	228
245	135	147	159	172	184	196	208	221	233
250	138	150	163	175	188	200	213	225	238
255	140	153	166	179	191	204	217	230	242
260	143	156	169	182	195	208	221	234	247
265	146	159	172	186	199	212	225	239	252
270	149	162	176	189	203	216	230	243	257
275	151	165	179	193	206	220	234	248	261
280	154	168	182	196	210	224	238	252	266
285	157	171	185	200	214	228	242	257	271
290	160	174	189	203	218	232	247	261	276
295	162	177	192	207	221	236	251	266	280
300	165	180	195	210	225	240	255	270	285
305	168	183	198	214	229	244	259	275	290
310	171	186	202	217	233	248	264	279	295
315	173	189	205	221	236	252	268	284	299
320	176	192	208	224	240	256	272	288	304
325	179	195	211	228	244	260	276	293	309
330	182	198	215	231	248	264	281	297	314
335	184	201	218	235	251	268	285	302	318
340	187	204	221	238	255	272	289	306	323
345	190	207	224	242	259	276	293	311	328
350	193	210	228	245	263	280	298	315	333
355	195	213	231	249	266	284	302	320	337
360	198	216	234	252	270	288	306	324	342
365	201	219	237	256	274	292	310	329	347
370	204	222	241	259	278	296	315	333	352

Max Load	55%	60%	65%	70%	75%	80%	85%	90%	95%
375	206	225	244	263	281	300	319	338	356
380	209	228	247	266	285	304	323	342	361
385	212	231	250	270	289	308	327	347	366
390	215	234	254	273	293	312	332	351	371
395	217	237	257	277	296	316	336	356	375
400	220	240	260	280	300	320	340	360	380
405	223	243	263	284	304	324	344	365	385
410	226	246	267	287	308	328	349	369	390
415	228	249	270	291	311	332	353	374	394
420	231	252	273	294	315	336	357	378	399
425	234	255	276	298	319	340	361	383	404
430	237	258	280	301	323	344	366	387	409
435	239	261	283	305	326	348	370	392	413
440	242	264	286	308	330	352	374	396	418
445	245	267	289	312	334	356	378	401	423
450	248	270	293	315	338	360	383	405	428
455	250	273	296	319	341	364	387	410	432
460	253	276	299	322	345	368	391	414	437
465	256	279	302	326	349	372	395	419	442
470	259	282	306	329	353	376	400	423	447
475	261	285	309	333	356	380	404	428	451
480	264	288	312	336	360	384	408	432	456
485	267	291	315	340	364	388	412	437	461
490	270	294	319	343	368	392	417	441	466
495	272	297	322	347	371	396	421	446	470
500	275	300	325	350	375	400	425	450	475
505	278	303	328	354	379	404	429	455	480
510	281	306	332	357	383	408	434	459	485
515	237	258	280	301	323	344	366	387	409